Literacy World Satellites

CW01651680

Stage 3

Reading and Language Skills Book

When you see this symbol it means you will need a copy of the book.

Heinemann

Contents

* Children will need to read the whole story/play before doing these activities.

What Are They Thinking?

In the scenes below, some of the characters do not speak. Find the scenes in the story. Write what the characters might be thinking.

1 What is Jodie thinking? (page 19)

2 What is Jodie thinking? (page 28)

3 What are Dr Baxter, Tom and Jodie thinking? (page 38)

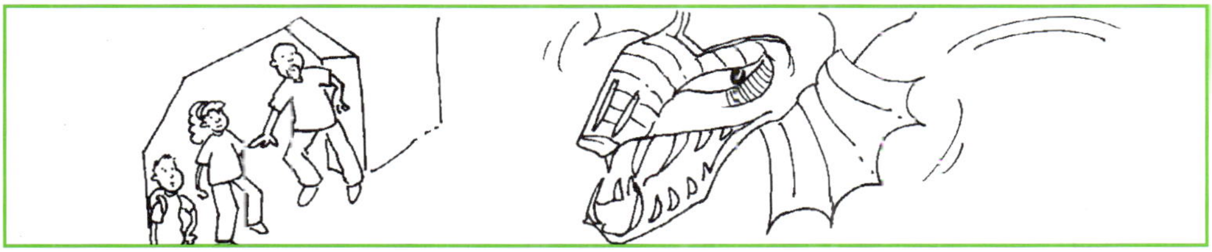

4 What is Professor Mace thinking? (page 46)

Speech Punctuation

Speech marks are used at the beginning and end of words which are spoken.

e.g. "I have something for you, Dr Baxter," said Mohammed.

Change the speech bubble text into sentences with speech marks. Add the correct speakers from the story.

1 page 8 — Come on, get ready. We're going on an adventure.

"Come on, get ready. We're going on an adventure," said Dr Baxter.

2 page 15 — You just want to keep the glory of its discovery for yourself!

3 page 25 — Dad, my torch is going out.

4 page 27 — I *hate* snakes!

5 page 32 — Now you are completely in my power!

6 page 46 — You should be *ashamed* of yourself.

Idioms

An **idiom** is an expression that has a different meaning to what the words suggest.
e.g. Professor Mace ***gets into hot water*** *in the story, which means he* ***gets into trouble****.*

Write out these idioms with their correct meanings from the box below.

1 to blow your own trumpet
to boast

2 to have a bee in your bonnet

3 to sit on the fence

4 to feel under the weather

5 to hold your tongue

6 to feather your own nest

7 to hit the nail on the head

8 to face the music

to avoid taking sides
to feel unwell
to be right
to look after yourself, not others
to be obsessed with an idea
~~to boast~~
to meet the worst
to keep silent

Writing New Scenes

In the story we see Professor Mace on page 41, but then we don't see him again until page 46, when he's outside the pyramid.

Write how you think Professor Mace got out of the pyramid. Use the frame below to help you.

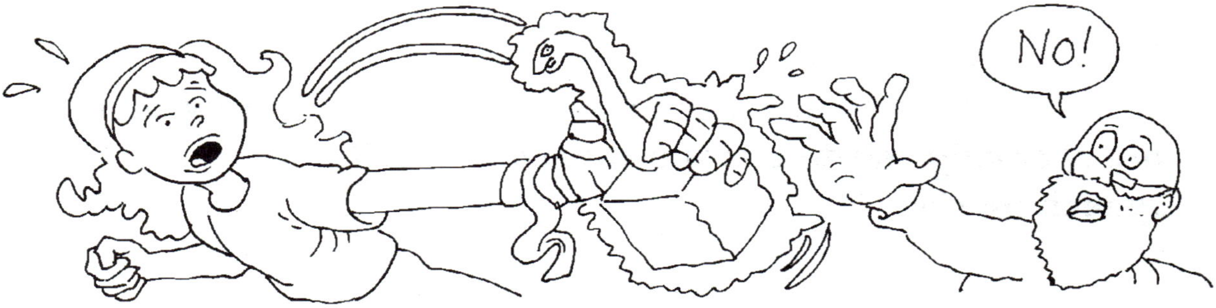

- Jodie grabs the **dark** cube from her father with her bandaged hand.
- Then Jodie and the others run for their lives.
- Meanwhile, Professor Mace ...
- Then ...
- To his surprise, Professor Mace ...

Adverbs to Describe Speech

Graphic novels have no **adverbs** to tell us **how** the characters are speaking, because speech bubbles only contain the actual words spoken.

e.g. *Thank you, Mohammed.*

Read the speech bubbles below. Decide who is speaking and choose an adverb from the box to describe how they are speaking. Write out the speeches in full using speech marks.

eagerly confidently desperately firmly ~~curiously~~

1 page 13 — What have you found?

"What have you found?" asked Tom curiously.

2 page 13 — Are we going inside?

3 page 15 — No. It stays *hidden*.

4 page 30 — What's wrong with him?

5 page 41 — *All* snakes are afraid of fire!

Leaving Words Out

In graphic novels, speech bubbles don't always show every word that might be written if the speeches were written out in full.

e.g. *More warnings.*

Written out in full this would be:
"Here are some more warnings," said Dr Baxter.

Read the speech bubbles below. Decide who is speaking and what words are missing. Write out the speeches in full using speech marks.

1 page 22 Can't reach …

"I can't reach you," said Jodie.

2 page 23 Lucky escape!

3 page 27 Snakes!

4 page 35 Got it!

5 page 39 Jodie, wait.

6 page 45 Jodie?

Finding Evidence

Complete the sentences by finding the words the characters say in the play.

1 Aso is bossy when she says, *"Go on then! Go in!"* (page 5)

2 The Sky God flatters Anansi when he says … (page 7)

3 Hornet is cruel when he says … (page 9)

4 Aso is confident when she says … (page 10)

5 Python is impatient when he says … (page 15)

6 Python is worried when he says … (page 16)

7 Leopard is desperate when he says … (page 23)

8 Anansi is triumphant when he says … (page 24)

Plurals

Most words form the **plural** by adding **-s**, but words which end in **-ch**, **-sh**, **-s**, **-x** and **-z** form the plural by adding **-es**.

e.g. *hiss* ⟶ *hisses*
buzz ⟶ *buzzes*

A ***Write the plurals of these words.***

trick	stitch	shop	school	tree
pitch	sister	box	girl	patch
bush	bus	watch	spider	lunch
fish	kiss	game	dish	glass

B ***How many more words can you find that form the plural by adding -es? Make a list.***

Comprehension

Answer these questions about Birbal's Trick.

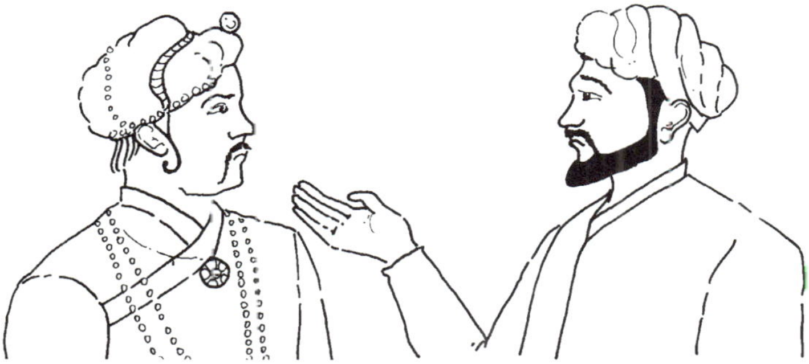

1 Why didn't Vikra want Birbal to be Akbar's chief advisor? (page 26)

2 What challenge did Akbar set Birbal and Tansen? (page 30)

3 What were Birbal and Tansen arguing about? (page 35)

4 Why was the King of Burma surprised? (page 35)

5 What did Birbal say Akbar wanted from the King of Burma? (page 37)

6 What did Birbal say was Akbar's reason for having them killed? (page 38)

7 What reason did Birbal give for the argument over who should die first? (page 40)

8 Why did the King of Burma set Birbal and Tansen free? (page 40)

Describing Characters

A ***Read the phrases below. Do they describe Birbal or Tansen? Write the phrases which describe Birbal under his name. Do the same for Tansen.***

- very talented
- not of noble birth
- the cleverest man I know
- poor and humble
- from a rich and noble family
- a great musician

B ***Think of four words or phrases to describe Akbar and write them under his name. Do the same for the King of Burma.***

e.g. ***Akbar***
wise

e.g. ***The King of Burma***
angry

Writing a Playscript

On page 57 of* Kahu's Trick, *the taniwha captures Koka and carries her to his cave. Continue the conversation between the taniwha and Koka as a playscript.

Koka *(Terrified)* Help! Help!

Taniwha There is no help for you. You cannot escape and no one can harm me. Wait until Kahu comes along and I tell him about this prize.

Koka ______________________________

Taniwha ______________________________

Koka ______________________________

Taniwha ______________________________

Koka ______________________________

Taniwha ______________________________

Wanted Poster

Create a Wanted Poster for the taniwha. Don't forget to include:

- his appearance
- his character
- where he lives
- what he likes
- his favourite meal
- what he cannot be killed by.

Misunderstandings

A *Complete the sentences to explain the misunderstandings in the story.*

1. The tiger thinks that the drip-drip-drip is …
2. The farmer thinks that the tiger is …
3. The tiger thinks that the farmer is …
4. The king thinks that the farmer is …
5. The soldiers think that the farmer is …

B *What was really happening in the story? Answer these questions.*

1. What was the drip-drip-drip?
2. Why did the farmer ride on a tiger?
3. Was the farmer really brave?

Powerful Verbs

Verbs are doing words. They tell us what people, animals or things do.
e.g. The tiger ***didn't like*** *getting wet and cold.*

Powerful **verbs** make sentences more interesting.
e.g. The tiger ***hated*** *getting wet and cold.*

A *Write out the sentences, replacing the underlined verbs with the powerful verbs used in the story.*

1 The tiger went up to the wall of a small house where it could shelter. (page 4)

2 A woman was calling at the top of her voice. (page 4)

3 "Stop it! Stop it!" the woman called. (page 4)

4 The donkey had run off into the storm and the farmer was looking for it. (page 6)

5 "Ah-hah!" the farmer said, holding the tiger by the ear. (page 7)

B *Change the verbs in the box to powerful verbs and use them in sentences of your own.*

got	said	went

e.g. He ***got*** *first prize.* → *He* ***won*** *first prize.*

Characteristics of Traditional Tales

Many traditional tales have similar characteristics. Which of the characteristics below occur in* The Princess and the Flea*? Write a list.

- There is a beautiful princess.
- The princess is the youngest of three sisters.
- The princess has a cruel step-father.
- The hero is poor.
- The hero is very clever.
- The hero is set a challenge.
- The hero helps an animal which is in trouble.
- The hero helps someone and is rewarded.
- The reward is gold and silver.
- At first the princess does not like the hero.
- The hero marries the princess.

Limericks

Limericks are poems of five lines.
Lines 1, 2 and 5 rhyme and lines 3 and 4 rhyme.

e.g.
There was a young man from Bengal.
Who went to a fancy-dress ball.
He thought he would risk it
and went as a biscuit.
But a dog ate him up in the hall.

Complete these limericks. Use the rhyming words in the boxes to help you.

fee key knee pea sea tea three tree
grey hay lay may pay play say way

The Princess had a pet flea.

____

It grew bigger each day

____

____

bad dad glad had mad pad sad
door floor four more raw saw

Chico was a clever young lad.

____

He blew down the straw

____

____

Expanding Sentences

Sentences can be **expanded** to make them more interesting.

e.g. *Timmy was a lad.* → *Timmy was a **clever** lad.*

→ *Timmy was a lad **who loved telling tall stories**.*

A *Use the words in the box to expand these sentences.*

tall	very	terrible	huge

1. Timmy loved to tell stories.
2. There was a tall cherry tree.
3. A storm started howling.
4. The cook was cutting up a turnip.

B *Use the phrases in the box to expand these sentences.*

nailed to a tree	just in time
as big as a football	at that very moment

1. Timmy saw a poster.
2. The cook was cutting up a turnip.
3. She held out her apron and she caught me.
4. A big fish was swimming by.

Plurals

Most words ending in **-f** or **-fe** change the **-f** or **-fe** to **-ves** when they become **plural**.

e.g. *loaf* → *loaves*
knife → *knives*

A *Write the plurals of these words.*

leaf wolf scarf life half
thief shelf calf wife

B *Write out the sentences, adding the correct plural words.*

1 The King's cook had several sharp ________ in his kitchen.

2 The ________ on the trees were bright green.

3 Cats have nine ________.

4 The ________ were caught stealing the money.

5 Two ________ make one whole.

6 The books were put away on the ________.

7 The children put on their hats, gloves and ________ before going outside.

Characters' Problems

Answer these questions about Foul Play.

1 Who is frightened of Shane? (page 9)

2 Who is jealous of Tim's success? (page 10)

3 Who is worried that Alice might be bullied at Leafield? (page 14)

4 Who is worried about what will happen to Tim and Alice at Leafield? (page 16)

5 Who is worried about where Tim is? (page 24)

6 Who is worried that Leafield will win the match? (page 30)

7 Who is worried that Tim will miss the match? (page 32)

8 Who is upset at being blamed for Tim's disappearance? (page 41)

Football Vocabulary

Copy and complete the table. Write the words from the box next to the correct definitions. Write your own definitions for the other words.

dribble touchline kick off striker

Football term	**Definition**
goalie	
	the start of the match
	to tap the football forward with the foot
half time	
referee	
	lines marking out the pitch
tackle	
	goal-scoring player

The Character of Shane

A ***At the beginning of* Foul Play*, Shane is a bully. Look at the following pages and write out the evidence.***

page 11

page 13

page 14

page 23

At the end of the story, Shane seems less of a bully. What evidence is there that he has changed? Look at the following pages and write out the evidence.

page 46

page 47

B ***Is Shane a bully? What do you think?***

I think …

Adverbs to Describe Speech

Adverbs can be used to describe **how** a character is speaking.

e.g. "Goal!" shouted Alice ***excitedly****.*

Read the sentences below. Decide who is speaking and choose an adverb from the box to describe how they are speaking. Write out the completed sentences.

bravely	kindly	~~confidently~~
anxiously	unkindly	angrily

1 "You don't scare me," said _______ _______. (page 13)

"You don't scare me," said Tim confidently.

2 "I won't let a bully like him spoil things," said _______ _______. (page 15)

3 "Chicken!" whispered _______ _______. (page 23)

4 "I bet it was Shane," said _______ _______. (page 35)

5 "I didn't want Shane to bully you," said _______ _______. (page 44)

6 "I don't think there will be any more problems from Shane," said _______ _______. (page 47)

Punctuating a Conversation

Read the speech bubble conversations below.
Write out the conversations using speech marks.

"Where's the star goalie, then?" asked Shane.
"He's . . .

Verb Tenses

Verbs in the **present tense** tell you what is happening **now**.
e.g. Shane ***kicks*** *the football into the goal.*

Verbs in the **past tense** tell you what has happened in the **past**.
e.g. Shane ***kicked*** *the football into the goal.*

A ***Copy and complete the table of present tense and past tense verbs.***

Present tense	Past tense
plays	
	laughed
	raced
shouts	
bounces	
	scored
cheers	
	pushed
scares	
	scratched

B ***Write out these sentences, changing the present tense verbs into the past tense.***

1 Alice looks at Billy and smiles at him.

2 Shane laughs at Tim and walks off.

3 Tim heads the ball and Spiky kicks it into the goal.

Double Negatives

Negative words are: **no, not, never, nothing, nowhere** and words with **n't** in them.
*e.g. I **can't** see any volcanoes.*

If you put two **negative** words in the same sentence they cancel each other out, and the sentence means the opposite of what was intended!

*e.g. I **can't** see **no** volcanoes.* means *I **can** see **some** volcanoes.*

The correct sentence should only have one **negative** word.
*i.e. I **can't** see **any** volcanoes.*

Write out these sentences, replacing the second negative word with a new word so that the sentences make sense.

1 I **can't** see **nothing** in this smoke.
*I **can't** see **anything** in this smoke.*

2 We're not going nowhere now.

3 I've not got no strength left.

4 I don't think I can go no further.

5 I can't get no sound from the radio.

6 The helicopter will not rescue nobody.

Changing Tenses

Verbs describe actions that are taking place **now, in the past** or **in the future**.

e.g. *I* ***escaped*** *from the burning crater. (past tense)*

I am ***escaping*** *from the burning crater. (present tense)*

I will ***escape*** *from the burning crater. (future tense)*

A ***Sort the verbs in the box into three lists, using these headings:***

present tense **past tense** **future tense**

writing felt will find took will take
driving broke breaking will drive
drove spoke wrote will speak
found taking speaking will write
will break finding will feel feeling

B ***Change these present tense sentences into the past tense and then into the future tense.***

1 I am dressing quickly.

2 I am leaving the house.

3 I am walking to school.

4 I am looking for my friends.

Point of View

Imagine you are Clare's mum. You hear the news of the bus crash on the local radio. Describe how you feel and what you do. Use the frame below to help you.

- I was just about to leave the house for work when I heard the news on the radio. At first …
- I drove as quickly as I dared …
- When I arrived at the scene of the accident …
- A policewoman …
- I heard somebody say …
- Then I saw Clare's friend, Nina …
- At last I saw Clare …

Apostrophe for Possession

An **apostrophe** shows that something belongs to somebody.

To show that something belongs to **one person** add **'s**. *e.g. the girl**'s** clothes*

To show that something belongs to **more than one person** add **'**. *e.g. the girls**'** clothes*

A *Rewrite these phrases using apostrophes.*

1 the brakes of the coach → *the coach's brakes*

2 the back of the driver

3 the cries of the girls

4 the siren of the fire engine

B *Write the correct phrase for each picture.*

1 the boy's bikes
the boys' bikes

2 the teacher's books
the teachers' books

C *Can you find any exceptions to the apostrophe rules above?*

Recording Reflections

How did you feel when you read about the earthquake in Mexico City? Write about how you felt when:

1 You first read about the earthquake.
When I first read about the earthquake I …

2 Pedro sees the cars rising and falling like boats on a rough sea.
When Pedro saw the cars I …

3 Pedro crawls out from underneath the car.
When Pedro crawled out from under the car …

4 Pedro thinks his parents have been killed.
When Pedro thought his parents had been killed I …

5 Elsa is dug out from the rubble.
When Elsa was dug out from the rubble I …

'ie' or 'ei'

When **ie** or **ei** sound like **ee** in **feet**, then **i** comes before **e** except after **c**.

This little rhyme might help you:

When the sound is like **ee**, *then it's* **i** *before* **e**, *except after* **c**.

A ***Write out these words putting* ie *or* ei *in the gaps.***

bel _ _ ve	gr _ _ f	rec _ _ ve	sh _ _ ld
ch _ _ f	rec _ _ pt	dec _ _ ve	p _ _ ce

When **ie** and **ei** do not make the **ee** sound then **e** comes before **i**.

B ***Write out these words adding* ei. *What sound does the* ei *make in each word?***

w _ _ ght	v _ _ n	h _ _ ght
n _ _ ghbour	_ _ ght	

The exception to these rules is **friend**.

C ***Spell the word* friend *six times using* look, say, cover, write, check.**